SPARKY'S STEM GUIDE TO...
CARS

BY KIRSTY HOLMES

©2019
The Secret Book Company
King's Lynn
Norfolk PE30 4LS

All rights reserved.
Printed in Malaysia.

A catalogue record for this book is available from the British Library.

ISBN: 978-1-78998-059-2

Written by:
Kirsty Holmes

Edited by:
Emilie Dufresne

Designed by:
Danielle Rippengill

All facts, statistics, web addresses and URLs in this book were verified as valid and accurate at time of writing. No responsibility for any changes to external websites or references can be accepted by either the author or publisher.

Original idea by Harrison Holmes.

IMAGE CREDITS

*All images are courtesy of Shutterstock.com, unless otherwise specified. With thanks to Getty Images, Thinkstock Photo and iStockphoto.
Cover – NotionPic, A–R–T, logika600, BiterBig, miniaria, Macrovector. Sparky – NotionPic, Macrovector. Peggy – NotionPic. Grid – BiterBig.
Driving School – Mascha Tace. 2 – Viktor96. 5 – Mascha Tace. 6 – miniaria, EgudinKa, Ivan Paal. 7 – studioworkstock, Viktor96. 8 & 9 – Viktor96.
10 – Pretty Vectors. 11 – Viktor96. 12 – VectorMine. 13 – miniaria, Mascha Tace. 14 – Fleren. 15 – VoodooDot, RedKoala. 16 & 17 – Wth. 18 – Mascha Tace,
VectorShow, miniaria. 19 – Igogosha. 20 – Mascha Tace. 22 – Alexandr III, Icon Craft Studio. 23 – Viktor96, GraphicsRF.*

CONTENTS

PAGE 4	Welcome to Driving School!
PAGE 6	Lesson 1: What Is a Car?
PAGE 8	Lesson 2: Parts of a Car
PAGE 10	Lesson 3: Inside a Car
PAGE 12	Lesson 4: Engines!
PAGE 14	Lesson 5: Safety!
PAGE 16	Lesson 6: The Need for Speed!
PAGE 18	Lesson 7: Cool Cars
PAGE 20	Driving Test
PAGE 22	Bonus Lesson: The Ring of Fire!
PAGE 24	Glossary and Index

WORDS THAT LOOK LIKE THIS CAN BE FOUND IN THE GLOSSARY ON PAGE 24.

WELCOME TO DRIVING SCHOOL!

HELLO! I'm Jeremy Sparkplug, world-famous racing driver. You can call me Sparky. You must be the new recruits. Welcome to the Horses for Courses School of Motoring!

Here you will be learning about some of the coolest **VEHICLES** on four wheels. If you pass your driving test, you'll earn your Golden Horseshoe. So pay attention: it's time to DRIVE!

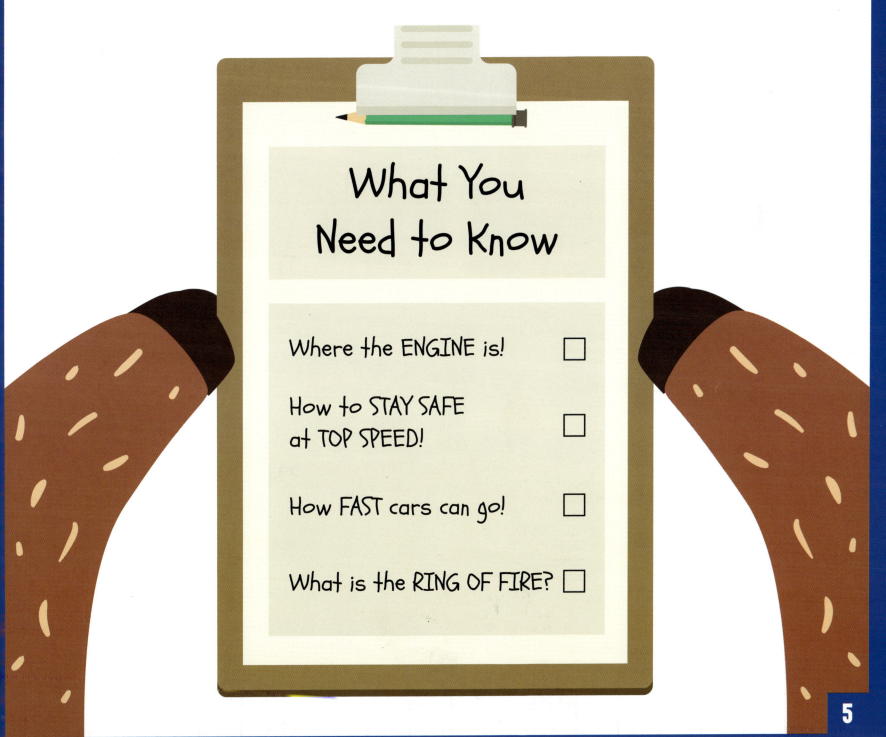

What You Need to Know

- Where the ENGINE is! ☐
- How to STAY SAFE at TOP SPEED! ☐
- How FAST cars can go! ☐
- What is the RING OF FIRE? ☐

Lesson 1: What is a Car?

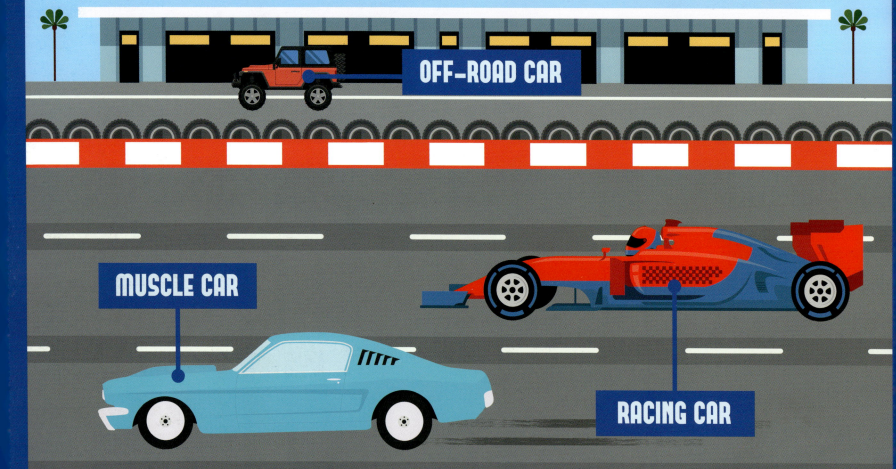

OFF-ROAD CAR

MUSCLE CAR

RACING CAR

A car is a type of **PASSENGER** vehicle. Cars run mostly on roads, can seat up to eight people and usually have four wheels.

Lesson 2: PARTS OF A CAR

WING MIRRORS
Drivers use these to see behind them.

TYRES
Tyres are made of **RUBBER**. A special pattern, called a tread, helps the tyres to grip the road.

"Let's look at the parts of a car."

ENGINE
The engine uses **FUEL** to create energy to power the car.

LIGHTS
These are for driving at night and to show when you are turning or stopping.

CARS ARE ALL DIFFERENT, BUT WILL HAVE THESE SAME BASIC PARTS.

WINDSCREEN
This is a glass window at the front of the car.

EXHAUST
Any waste **GASES** come out here.

BUMPERS
These stop low-speed accidents from causing too much damage.

NUMBER PLATES
This shows a special code that is different for each car.

9

Lesson 3: INSIDE A CAR

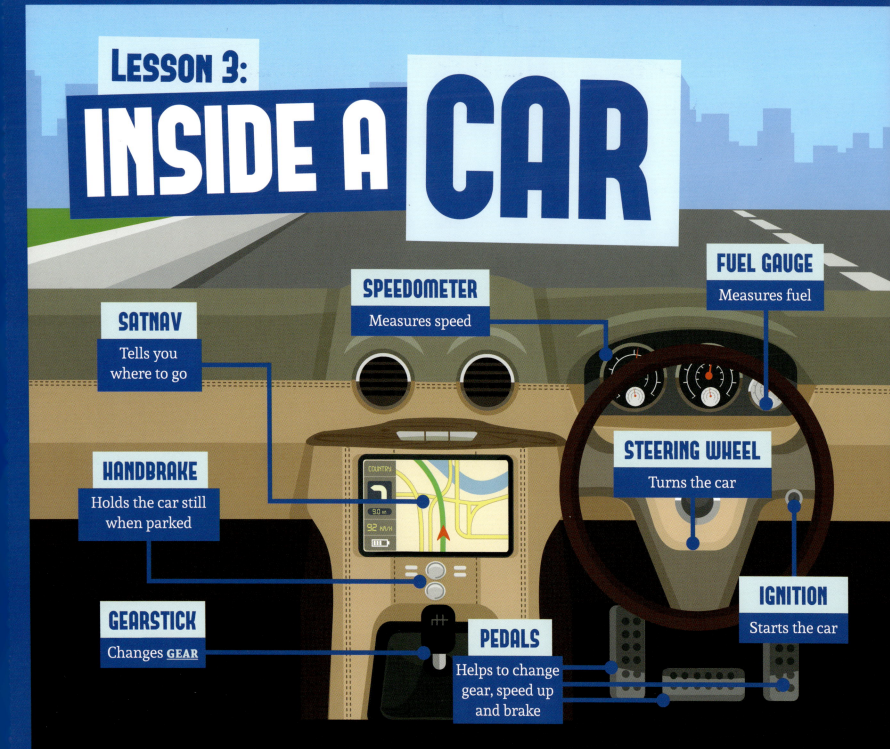

Inside a car, there are controls on the DASHBOARD and on the floor by the driver. There are also INSTRUMENTS which give the driver important information.

The driver sits on the right-hand side in some countries, and on the left-hand side in others. The driver's seat is usually on the opposite side to the side of the road they drive on, so the driver is nearer the middle of the road.

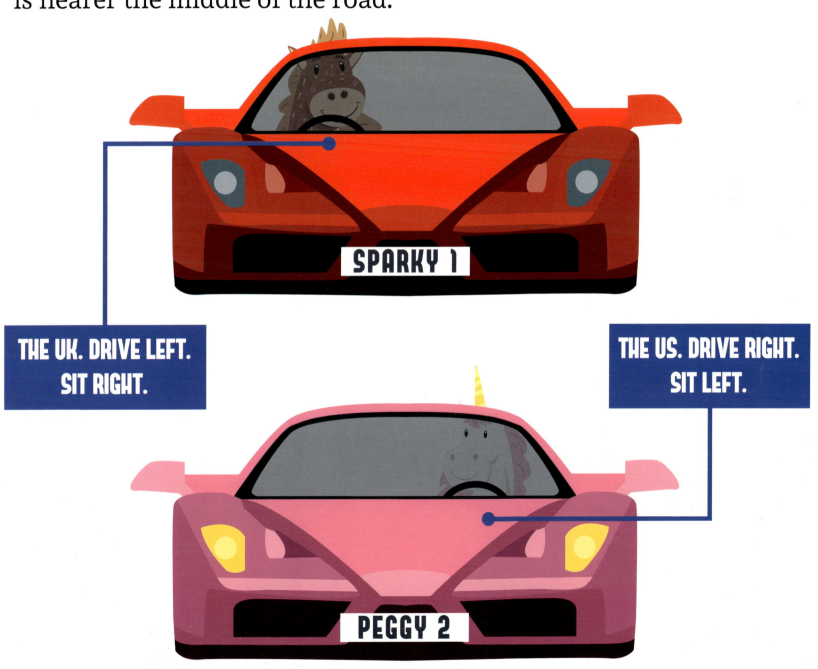

THE UK. DRIVE LEFT. SIT RIGHT.

THE US. DRIVE RIGHT. SIT LEFT.

Lesson 4:
ENGINES!

Combustion engines use small explosions from fuel to make **pistons** move up and down. This makes the wheels turn.

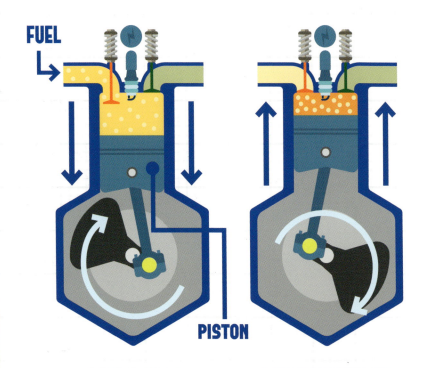

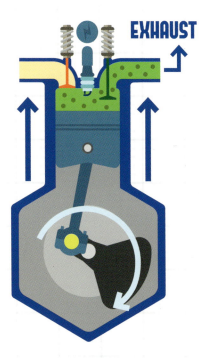

1. SUCK
Air and fuel go in.

2. SQUEEZE
The mixture is squashed.

3. BANG
A small explosion pushes the piston.

4. BLOW
Waste gases are pushed out.

An electric car is powered by an electric motor and a battery. These need to be charged up at a special socket, a bit like a mobile phone.

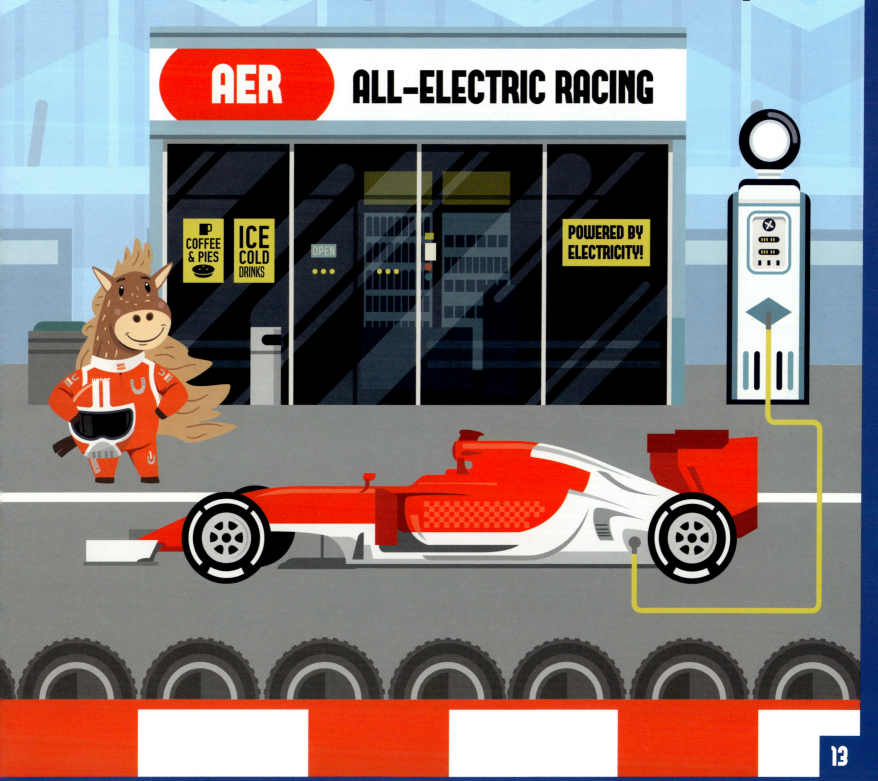

Lesson 5:
SAFETY!

Did you know that the first cars didn't have seatbelts? Don't worry – although nobody wants to be in a car accident, modern cars have lots of clever ways to keep us safe.

Take it from a racing driver like me: ALWAYS wear your seatbelt.

SAFETY FEATURES

AIRBAG
A bag inflates and stops you banging your head inside the car.

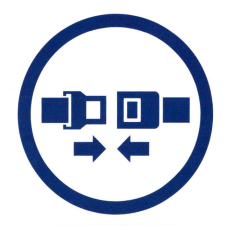

SEATBELT
A strap holds you in your seat in case there is a crash.

BABY CARRIERS
Babies should face backwards in a special car seat.

CHILD SEATS
Older children should use a booster seat until they are around 12.

HEAD RESTRAINTS
These protect your neck by stopping your head snapping back.

CRUMPLE ZONE
The front of the car squashes easily, so the passenger is protected.

Lesson 6: THE NEED FOR SPEED!

Some of the fastest cars around are the sleek, speedy race cars of **Formula 1** (F1) racing. They are built to be light, low to the ground and to be very aerodynamic. Let's look at what that means.

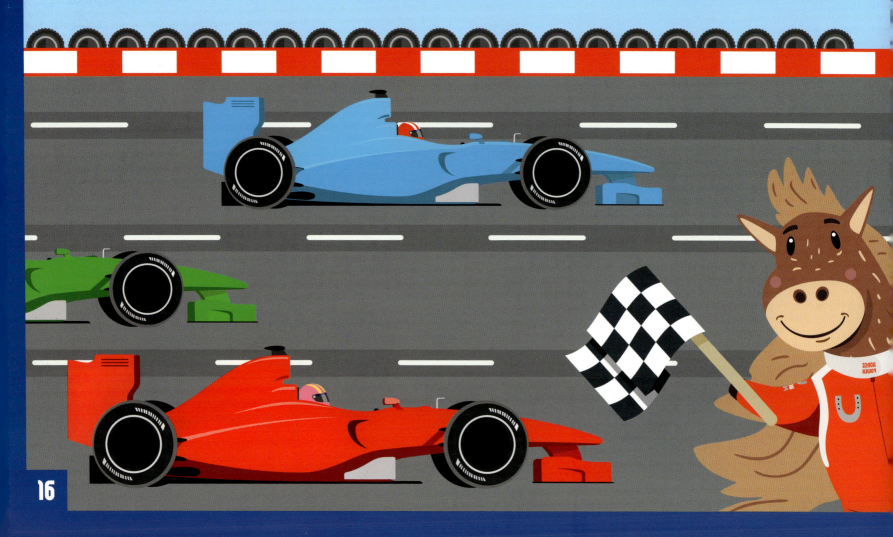

Because the car is so low, air can pass over the top and push the car towards the ground. The wedge-like shape helps the car cut through the air.

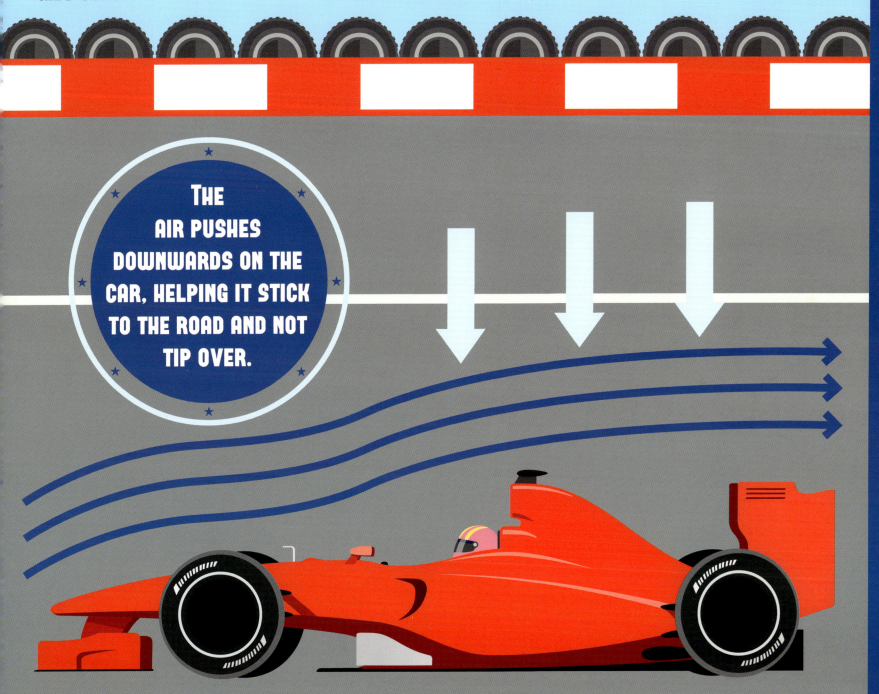

The air pushes downwards on the car, helping it stick to the road and not tip over.

Lesson 7: Cool Cars

Thrust SSC

The Thrust Supersonic Car has held the land speed record since 1997. It made a top speed of 1,227.985 kilometres per hour and was the first ever land vehicle to go faster than the speed of sound.

BAR-Honda 067 Lakester

The fastest F1 car ever, the 067 Lakester, reached 413 kilometres per hour.

Longest Car Ever

At 30.5 metres long, with 26 wheels, Jay Ohrberg's limousine holds the world record for the longest car. It has its own small swimming pool.

THE SMALLEST CAR

PEEL P50

The smallest road car ever made, the P50, was made for "one adult and a shopping bag". Only 50 were ever made.

DRIVING TEST

Buckle up, learners. Time to gallop through your driving test and see if you're an ace racer – or whether you've just been horsing around!

Questions

1. What are car tyres usually made of?

2. What does the ignition do?

3. What are the four stages in a combustion engine?

4. What should all passengers in a car always wear?

5. How fast was the Thrust SSC?

Did you get all the answers right?

Of course you did – here is your Golden Horseshoe.
You are now an ace racing driver, just like Peggy and me!

Answers: 1. Rubber 2. Starts the engine 3. Suck, squeeze, bang, blow 4. A seatbelt 5. 1,227.985 kilometres per hour

Bonus Lesson:
THE RING OF FIRE!

Stunt drivers perform terrifying tricks and death-defying feats of daring in their cars. It takes years of training, but we're professionals, so let us show you how it's done...

STEP ONE
Get stunt car

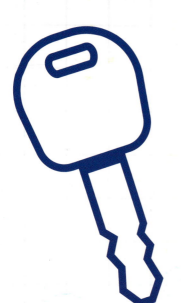

STEP TWO
Safety checks

STEP THREE
Matches

GLOSSARY

COMBUSTION — the act of burning or setting fire to something
DASHBOARD — the panel facing the driver of a vehicle, which contains the controls for driving
FORMULA 1 — a popular motor vehicle racing competition
FUEL — a material used to make heat or power
GASES — things that are like air, that fill any space available
GEAR — part of a machine that makes other parts move
INSTRUMENTS — devices that measure something, such as speed or the amount of fuel
PASSENGER — someone who rides in a vehicle but is not the driver
PISTONS — pieces of machinery that move up and down in a car engine
RUBBER — a bouncy material made from tropical plants
VEHICLES — machines used for carrying or transporting things or people

INDEX

ACCIDENTS 9, 14
COMBUSTION ENGINES 12, 20
DASHBOARDS 10
ELECTRIC CARS 13
FUEL 9–10, 12
LEFT-HAND 11
PASSENGERS 6, 15, 20
RIGHT-HAND 11
ROADS 6, 8, 11, 17, 19
STUNTS 22